Contents

How to say the words

Ancient Egyptians (Ayn-shunt Ee-jip-shuns)
archaeologist (ark-ee-ol-u-jist)
hieroglyphics (hi-row-glif-ix)
pharaohs (fare-ose)
pyramids (pir-a-mids)
Osiris (Os-eye-ris)
scribes (scr-eye-bs)
tombs (tooms)
Tutankhamun (Toot-an-car-moon)

The Secrets of the Egyptians

Marian Iseard

Published in association with The Basic Skills Agency

Hodder & Stoughton

Acknowledgements
Cover: Ron Watts/Corbis

Photos: pp 3, 22 © Bettmann/Corbis; p 7 © Richard T. Nowitz/Corbis; pp10, 13 © Charles & Josette Lenars/Corbis; p 17 © Erich Lessing/AKG London

Illustrations: pp 4, 5 © Sara Pruce; p 26 © Maureen Carter

Every effort has been made to trace copyright holders of material reproduced in this book. Any rights not acknowledged will be acknowledged in subsequent printings if notice is given to the publisher.

Orders; please contact Bookpoint Ltd, 39 Milton Park, Abingdon, Oxon OX14 4TD. Telephone (44) 01235 400414, Fax: (44) 01235 400454. Lines are open from 9.00–6.00, Monday to Saturday, with a 24 hour message answering service. Email address: orders@bookpoint.co.uk

British Library Cataloguing in Publication Data
A catalogue record for this title is available from the British Library

ISBN 0 340 80073 9

First published 2001
Impression number   10 9 8 7 6 5 4 3 2 1
Year   2007 2006 2005 2004 2003 2002 2001

Typeset by SX Composing DTP, Rayleigh, Essex.
Printed in Great Britain for Hodder & Stoughton Educational, a division of Hodder Headline Plc, 338 Euston Road, London NW1 3BH by Redwood Books, Trowbridge, Wiltshire.

1 Lost in Time

The Ancient Egyptians lived
thousands of years ago.
They were clever people.
They built temples and pyramids.
They built big cities.
Now, not much is left of their world.

For a long time we knew little about their lives.
Many secrets had been lost in time.
Why were the pyramids built?
Why did they mummify dead bodies?
What food did they eat?
What games did they play?
No one knew.

The things they had written
were hard to read.
It was like a secret code.
And no one could read it.

2   Cracking the Code

The Egyptians had scribes
who wrote everything down.
They wrote about wars.
About kings and queens.
About the lives of ordinary people.
About how they made things.

But their writing was in pictures.
The picture-writing is called hieroglyphics.
To find out about their lives,
we had to learn how to read their picture-writing.

In 1799 some French soldiers
found the Rosetta Stone.
It had pictures and writing on it –
the same thing in both Egyptian and Greek.
We could start to understand
the secrets in the pictures.

Today, the Rosetta Stone is in the British Museum.

The Rosetta Stone helped us to understand Egyptian picture-writing.

3 Picture Stories

We can tell stories using pictures.
The Egyptians used pictures to show objects.
Here you can see the pictures
for water, pool and snake.

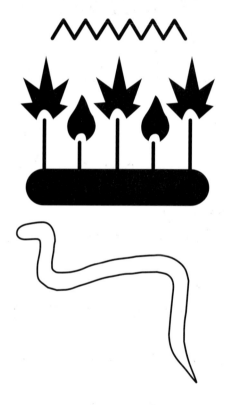

But pictures can only tell us so much.
Think about how you would say this:
'Don't go near the pool, there is a snake by the water.'

Like this?

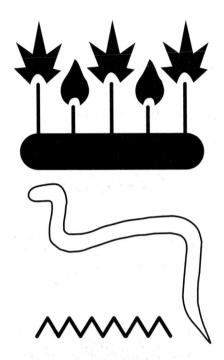

You could be saying,
'Go to the pool and fetch me some water,
there are no snakes.'
A deadly mistake!
So the Egyptians had signs, as well as pictures.

For example, this picture means 'mouth'.

But with a little line underneath it means 'towards'.
It was the start of a written language.

4 Digging up the Past

Another way for us to find out about the past
is to dig it up!
Archaeologists do this.
They dig where they think buildings might lie
under the ground.
In Egypt, the sun and the sand
have destroyed lots of ancient buildings.
Some were destroyed in battles.
Not much is left to find.

The one thing that was left was the dead.
Archaeologists found tombs –
tombs of kings and their families.
Inside the tombs there were many things.
On the walls there were pictures
and picture-writing.
These told stories from the past,
about the lives of kings.

Archaeologists have to be very careful when digging up ancient objects.

5   When a King Died

In Ancient Egypt,
the people called their kings Pharaohs.
The people believed that when the Pharaohs died
they became gods.
Their spirits would travel to the land of the dead.
This was ruled by Osiris, God of the dead.

One day, the body would join
the spirit in the after-life.
People buried the Pharaohs with all the things
they would need in the after-life.
Things like weapons, clothes and jewels.
Like games, food and wine.
Even beds and boats.
A lot of these things were made of gold.

So, the Pharaohs were buried
with all their treasure.
But first they had to be made ready
for the after-life.
They had to be made into mummies.

6 Mummies

It seems very strange to us
– to mummify a dead body.
But the Egyptians had seen what hot sand
did to dead bodies.
When a body was buried in hot sand it dried out.
It didn't rot away.

The Egyptians had the idea
of doing this to themselves.
But they didn't use sand to dry the body –
they used salt.
They became very good at mummifying bodies.
Only poor people were not mummified.
They were still buried in rags.

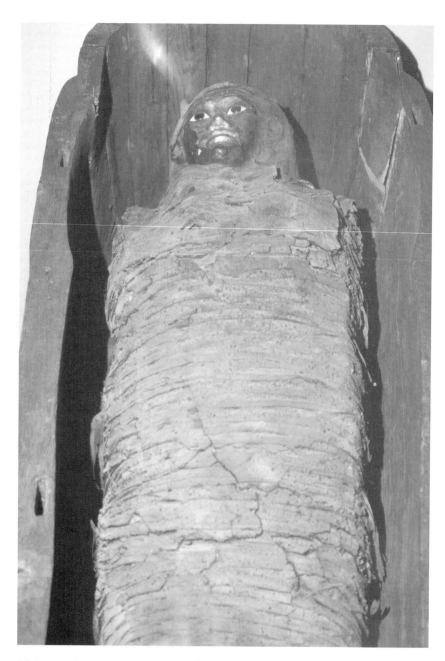

This ancient mummy is in his burial cask.

7   Making a Mummy

It took 70 days to mummify a body.
First, they made a hole in the skull
to take out the brains.
Then they took out everything from inside the body.
Only the heart was left.
Next they cleaned the body.

Then it was covered with a sort of salt called Natron.
This dried the body, just like hot sand.
It took 40 days to dry out.
If bits of fingers or toes fell off,
they put wooden ones on.
Then they wrapped the body in cloth,
and made a death-mask.
At last the body was ready for its coffin –
and the tomb.

8 Pyramids

The tombs of the first Pharaohs were pyramids.
People made the pyramids from blocks of stone.
Imagine dragging those huge stones in the hot sun.
We think that it took 100,000 men
25 years to build some of the bigger pyramids!
It was hard work.

First they had to cut the stone.
Then they moved the stones
by dragging them on wooden sledges,
or by sailing them on boats on the River Nile.

The workers were paid
with food, wine and clothes.
Some of them were slaves.
They worked for nothing.

The Egyptians used tools that we still use today,
like chisels and drills.
They used dishes of water
to check that the stones were level.
They sometimes used the stars
to help work out angles.

The Egyptians buried their Pharoahs in pyramids.

9   Hidden Treasure

The entrance to a pyramid was hidden.
Inside it was like a maze.
There were dead ends and secret passages.
The coffin lay in a room
with all the Pharaoh's treasures.
The door to this room was covered
by huge stone slabs.

It is hard to believe that anyone could get inside.
But some did –
men who took huge risks to get at the gold.
Men who stole everything
they could lay their hands on . . . tomb raiders.

10 Tomb Raiders!

A tomb raider risked his life to get at the treasure.
After all, the tombs were protected by the Gods.
He might be cursed by a God.
More likely, he might be caught.
And there was only one sentence – death.
(Death for a tomb raider
meant being crushed on a sharp spike.)
But they wanted the gold and jewels.
They wanted to get rich.
They got through all the locks
and heavy stone doors.
Sometimes they gave the guards
money to let them in.
Then they stole things and sold them.
Many things have been lost like this.

11 Glittering gold

On page 17 you can see some of the treasures
that the raiders might have found.
The raiders would have had candles to see inside.
The gold and jewels would have shone
in the candlelight.
It must have looked a wonderful sight.

Because of the tomb raiders
many of these things have been lost forever.
They had been sold, or destroyed.

This wooden box contains jewellery and cosmetic containers found in the tomb of an Egyptian girl.

12 Hiding the Dead

To fool the tomb raiders
some Pharaohs had secret tombs made.
These were in a valley
called The Valley of the Kings.
The tombs were cut into the cliffs
at the side of the valley.
They were guarded day and night.
But still the robbers found them.

What could people do?
The royal priests knew
they had to keep the Pharaoh mummies safe.
They thought up a plan.
It worked so well
that no-one knew anything about it
for many, many years . . .

13 The 3000-year-old Secret

Imagine hiding something
that you don't want anyone to find.

You carry it up a steep mountain.
You drag it down a narrow and very deep hole.
You carry it along a tunnel into the mountain.
At last you come to a big cave inside the mountain.
This is where you leave it.

It sounds like a fantasy film.
But this is just what the royal priests did.
It was about 1000 years BC.
The secret objects were the Pharaoh mummies.

The priests took the mummies from their tombs.
Then they buried them all together,
in the secret mountain cave.

The mummies stayed hidden – forgotten.
They were not found until 1881 – 3000 years later!

14 More Secrets

Archaeologists found more hidden mummies.
They opened tombs.
Most of these had been robbed,
but not everything had been taken.
Some treasure went to museums.
Some stayed in the tombs for visitors to see.

By 1920 people thought
there were no more secrets in
the Valley of the Kings.
But a man called Howard Carter
was sure there was one more tomb.
He kept looking.

In 1922 he found what he was looking for.
It was the tomb of Tutankhamun.
He was called the Boy King.

15 The Boy King

Tutankhamun was just 17 when he died.
He was only king for a short time.
And yet his tomb was full of treasure.
Raiders had got inside twice,
but had never taken much.
Someone may have heard them.
Maybe they ran off in a hurry.

For Howard Carter it was the find of his life.
He was the first to see inside the tomb,
through a small hole.
Someone asked him what he could see.
'Wonderful things,' he said.

Tutankhamun's mummy and all the fantastic treasure
are now in the Cairo Museum in Egypt.

The coffin of Tutankhamun.

16 The Curse of Tutankhamun

After Howard Carter's team opened
the tomb of Tutankhamun,
people started talking about a curse.

The man who had paid for the work suddenly died.
Some of the Egyptian workers
thought it was a curse.
They said he pricked his finger
on some treasure that had been cursed.
If anyone fell ill, or died,
people said it was the 'Curse of Tutankhamun'.

Even though Howard Carter lived to be 66
many people still believed in the curse.

Hollywood loved the story of the curse!
They made lots of horror films with mummies in.

17 Working Life in Egypt

The royal tombs made it easier for us
to find out about the lives of the kings.
But for everyone else what was life like?
Hard work, unless you were royal, or rich.
Most people were poor.
Not many knew how to read and write.

Most people had very hard jobs.
They worked on the land
or built new towns and villages.
Some were soldiers or craftsmen.
Only the boys of rich families went to school.
They would become doctors, or scribes, or priests.

Most women stayed at home,
looking after the house and the land.
A few worked as dancers and singers.

18 A Life in Pictures

Now we know so much more
about the Ancient Egyptians.
Look at the wall paintings on page 26.
They show how the people lived –
what they ate, what they wore,
what games they played, and many other things.